Coffee And A Good Friend Is The Best Therapy
Pretty Turquoise Journal for Coffee Lovers
Coffee Lover Gift Ideas for Women
Paperback ISBN: 978-1-989733-24-0
Published by Dunhill Clare Publishing 2020
 Cover Design by Sharon Purtill